MIAMI HEAT

ALL-TIME GREATS

BY TED COLEMAN

Book design by Jake Slavik
Cover design by Jake Slavik

Photographs ©: Marta Lavandier/AP Images, cover (top), 1 (top), 20; Duane Burleson/Paul Sancya/AP Images, cover (bottom), 1 (bottom); Al Messerschmidt/AP Images, 4; Mark Lennihan/AP Images, 7; Michael Caulfield/AP Images, 8; David J. Phillip/AP Images, 10; John Bazemore/AP Images, 13; Lynne Sladky/AP Images, 14; Michael Conroy/AP Images, 16; Matt Slocum/AP Images, 19

Press Box Books, an imprint of Press Room Editions.

ISBN
978-1-63494-603-2 (library bound)
978-1-63494-621-6 (paperback)
978-1-63494-639-1 (epub)
978-1-63494-655-1 (hosted ebook)

Library of Congress Control Number: 2022942568

Distributed by North Star Editions, Inc.
2297 Waters Drive
Mendota Heights, MN 55120
www.northstareditions.com

Printed in the United States of America
Mankato, MN
012023

ABOUT THE AUTHOR

Ted Coleman is a freelance sportswriter and children's book author who lives in Louisville, Kentucky, with his trusty Affenpinscher, Chloe.

TABLE OF CONTENTS

RICE
41

CHAPTER 1
WARMING UP

One of the first players in Miami Heat history was **Grant Long**. The Heat chose the power forward in their first NBA Draft in 1988. For six seasons he brought scoring from short range and rebounding. Long was a steady player on a struggling expansion team.

The Heat got a little better with the 1989 draft. The team badly needed offense. No team had scored fewer points per game in 1988–89. Forward **Glen Rice** helped change that.

Rice had starred for the national champion University of Michigan. He brought those skills to Miami and became the team's first star. Rice led the Heat to their first two playoff appearances. He was a talented scorer from anywhere on the floor. Rice took and made a lot of threes.

Rice's best year came in 1994–95. He was one of the league's top scorers at more than 22 points per game. So fans were upset when the Heat traded him to the Charlotte Hornets.

It was hard to stay mad, though. That trade brought **Alonzo Mourning** to Miami. The towering center was just beginning a Hall of Fame career. He became one of the most important players in Heat history.

Mourning was a force on both offense and defense. In his first Heat season, he averaged more than 20 points and 10 rebounds per

MOURNING
33

game. He went on to win Defensive Player of the Year twice.

Running the Heat offense was point guard **Tim Hardaway**. Hardaway was a skilled passer and playmaker. He also had scoring ability of his own. He and Mourning led the

STAT SPOTLIGHT

CAREER THREE-POINTERS

HEAT TEAM RECORD

Tim Hardaway: 806

COACH RILEY

Nobody has been a part of the Heat longer than Pat Riley. Riley was hired as coach and team president in 1995. He coached until 2003, and again from 2005 to 2008. As of 2022, Riley was nearing three decades as president. Riley built the best teams in Heat history.

team all the way to the conference finals in 1997.

The Heat got a shock in 2002. Mourning had a kidney disease and missed the season. Guard **Eddie Jones** helped replace Mourning's production. Jones was a good scorer and defender. But the team just wasn't the same without its big man.

WADE
3

CHAPTER 2

THE BIG THREE

By 2003, the Heat had been out of the playoffs for two seasons. They used their draft pick that year on **Dwyane Wade**. The shooting guard was an instant star. He led the Heat back to the playoffs. Wade ended up being the best player in team history. And he took the team to new heights.

Other players helped Wade along the way. **Udonis Haslem** wasn't a star. However, the forward was a steady presence on the Heat for two decades. Haslem did a little of everything. He was also a great teammate.

STAT SPOTLIGHT

CAREER GAMES PLAYED

HEAT TEAM RECORD

Dwyane Wade: 948

Shaquille O'Neal was the first superstar the Heat brought in to play alongside Wade. The massive center arrived in 2004. He was practically unstoppable under the basket.

The Heat finally reached the NBA Finals in 2006. They had the help of Alonzo Mourning, who came back to the team. The Dallas Mavericks jumped to an early 2–0 series lead. But Wade led the Heat back to victory. He was the Finals Most Valuable Player (MVP).

ODD NUMBERS

The Heat have retired six jersey numbers in honor of great players. Five of them are Heat legends. The sixth belongs to Michael Jordan. But Jordan never played for the Heat. The Heat simply wanted to honor Jordan's great career when he retired for good in 2003.

HEAT
32
O'NEAL
32

A few years later, the Heat took the NBA by storm. Wade was already a superstar. In 2010, the team added two more. Forward **Chris Bosh** was a rebounding force. **LeBron James** could do just about everything.

Many believed he was the NBA's best player. And he proved that in Miami. James was the NBA MVP in 2012 and 2013.

The "Big Three" turned the Heat into a power. They made four NBA Finals in a row. Twice, in 2012 and 2013, Miami won. **Ray Allen** played a key role in the second one. He was already one of the best three-point shooters ever. In Game 6, he hit one of the most famous shots in NBA history. It helped the Heat come back and win the game in overtime. They won the series in Game 7.

The Big Three era lasted just four years. James left in the summer of 2014. But the memories lasted forever for Heat fans.

WHITESIDE
21
FANDUEL
HEAT
21

CHAPTER 3

STILL HOT

Dwyane Wade, Chris Bosh, and Udonis Haslem kept the Heat competitive. Young center **Hassan Whiteside** breathed new life into the team, too. Whiteside averaged double figures in points and rebounds in all five seasons with Miami. He led the NBA in blocks per game in 2015–16. And then he led the league in rebounds per game in 2016–17. But Whiteside never developed into an All-Star. And he was gone by 2019.

By then, Wade and Bosh were gone too. The Heat rebuilt quickly with a mix of veterans and young players.

STAT SPOTLIGHT

SINGLE-SEASON FIELD-GOAL PERCENTAGE

HEAT TEAM RECORD

Hassan Whiteside: .606 **(2015-16)**

Veteran **Goran Dragic** was a fan favorite. The guard could score and set up teammates. He made one All-Star team while in Miami.

Then there were young players like **Bam Adebayo**. The center didn't have a big impact in 2017–18. Two years later he was an All-Star. He turned into one of the best defensive players in the league. Guard **Tyler Herro** was the team's top draft pick in 2019. Herro rarely started. But he provided a scoring boost off the bench like few other players. He won Sixth Man of the Year in 2021–22. That award is given to the best bench player in the league each season.

Jimmy Butler needed no introduction. He was already a star when he arrived in 2019. After bouncing around the league, he found

BUTLER
22

a home in Miami. Butler played with great intensity. His teammates followed his lead. In 2020, Butler led a surprising run to the NBA Finals. Adebayo and Dragic both got hurt. So Butler stepped up his game. He averaged more than 25 points per game in the Finals. But it wasn't enough to beat the Los Angeles Lakers. Two years later, Butler almost did it again. The Heat fell just short of the Finals. But with a strong core, the forecast in Miami remained hot.

COACH SPOELSTRA

Erik Spoelstra had a tough job. He replaced legendary Heat coach Pat Riley in 2008. Spoelstra soon became a coaching star himself. His Heat teams won two NBA titles during the Big Three era. Miami remained competitive even after that. The 2020 NBA Finals were Spoelstra's fifth. He is by far the team leader in wins.

TIMELINE

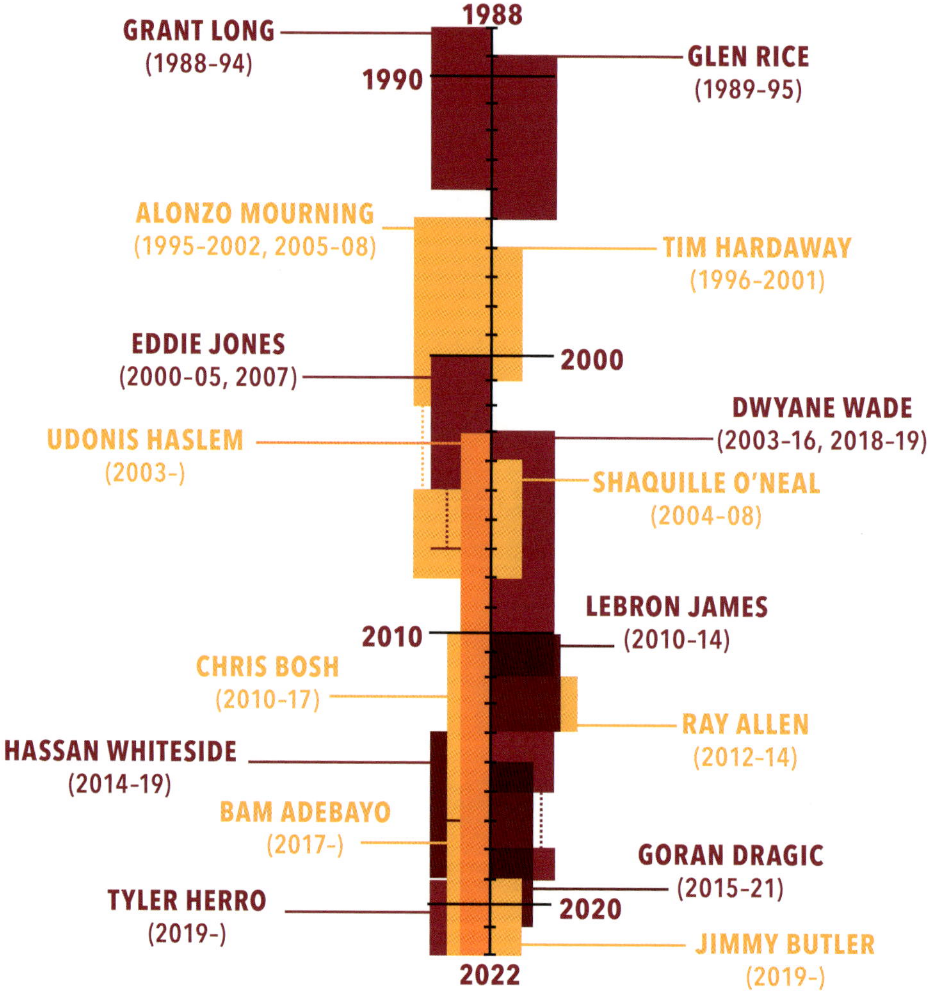
1988
GRANT LONG
(1988–94)
GLEN RICE
(1989–95)
1990
ALONZO MOURNING
(1995–2002, 2005–08)
TIM HARDAWAY
(1996–2001)
EDDIE JONES
(2000–05, 2007)
2000
DWYANE WADE
(2003–16, 2018–19)
UDONIS HASLEM
(2003-)
SHAQUILLE O'NEAL
(2004–08)
LEBRON JAMES
(2010–14)
2010
CHRIS BOSH
(2010–17)
RAY ALLEN
(2012–14)
HASSAN WHITESIDE
(2014–19)
BAM ADEBAYO
(2017-)
GORAN DRAGIC
(2015–21)
TYLER HERRO
(2019-)
2020
JIMMY BUTLER
(2019-)
2022

TEAM FACTS

MIAMI HEAT

First season: 1988–89

NBA championships: 3*

Key coaches:

Pat Riley (1995–96 to 2002–03, 2005–06 to 2007–08)

454–395, 34–36 playoffs, 1 NBA title

Erik Spoelstra (2008–09–)

660–453, 96–65 playoffs, 2 NBA titles

MORE INFORMATION

To learn more about the Miami Heat, go to **pressboxbooks.com/AllAccess.**

These links are routinely monitored and updated to provide the most current information available.

**Through 2021–22 season*

GLOSSARY

conference
A subset of teams within a sports league.

draft
A system that allows teams to acquire new players coming into a league.

era
A period of time in history.

expansion team
A new team that is added to an existing league.

playmaker
A player capable of setting up plays for others to score.

started
Played in a game from the beginning.

veterans
Players who have spent several years in a league.

INDEX